THE TALLEST

FASCINATING FACTS

David Armentrout

The Rourke Press, Inc.
Vero Beach, Florida 32964

PHOTO CREDITS
© Priscilla Eastman: pg. 4; © Kim Karpeles: Left Cover, pg. 10;
© James P. Rowan: Right Cover, Title page, pgs. 7, 12, 17, 21;
© David Rucker: pg. 13; © The Sand Sculpture Society, Harrison
Hot Springs, B. C.: pg. 18; © J. Robert Stottlemyer/Int'l Stock: pg.
15; © Hilary Wilkes/Int'l Stock: pg. 8

Library of Congress Cataloging-in-Publication Data

Armentrout, David, 1962–
    The tallest / by David Armentrout.
        p. cm. — (Fascinating facts)
    ISBN 1-57103-131-6
    Summary: Describes some of the tallest plants, animals,
geographic features, and man-made structures on earth.
    1. Curiosities and wonders—Juvenile literature. [1. Curiosities
and wonders.]
I. Title II. Series: Armentrout, David, 1962- Fascinating facts.
AG243.A63 1996
031.02—dc20   96–23861
                                               CIP
                                               AC

Printed in the USA

TABLE OF CONTENTS

MOUNTAIN PEAK

Mount Everest, in the Himalayan Mountains, towers over all other mountains in the world. Over 29,000 feet high, the peak of Mount Everest is the highest point on Earth.

People have always been fascinated by hard-to-reach mountain peaks. Hundreds of men and women have lost their lives in attempts to climb dangerous mountains.

Mount Everest claimed many lives before Sir Edmund Hillary and Tenzing Norgay made it to the top in 1953.

The peak of Mount Everest, the highest mountain in the world, rises above the clouds

ANIMAL

The giraffe is the tallest of all animals. Standing 18 feet, an adult giraffe is as tall as a two-story building.

Giraffes use their great height and keen sense of sight to keep watch for their main enemy, the lion. If startled by a hungry lion, a giraffe can run over 30 miles an hour.

These gentle giants get their food and most of their water by eating moist leaves from the tops of trees. In fact, a giraffe can go for over a month without drinking water.

The giraffe is tall enough to feed on leaves in the tops of trees

STATUE

The Statue of Liberty is the tallest statue in the United States. The statue is a women holding a book in her left hand and a torch raised high in her right hand. It stands on a small island in New York City's harbor, welcoming visitors to the United States.

Liberty was a gift from France in 1876, celebrating the 100th birthday of the U. S. The 152-foot statue has come to be a sign of freedom to people all over the world.

The Statue of Liberty is a major tourist attraction in the United States

SKYSCRAPER

Most large cities have tall buildings called skyscrapers. Skyscrapers are usually the first thing you see when you go near a city, because they can be seen from miles away. One of the tallest buildings in the world is Sears Tower in Chicago.

The Sears Tower was built between 1970 and 1974 for Sears, Roebuck and Company. The building is 1,454 feet tall and has 110 stories, or floors. A deck on top of the Sears Tower offers a view of the city below.

The 110-story Sears Tower has an observation deck where visitors go to view Chicago

The tallest of all monuments is "Gateway to the West" Arch in St. Louis

Yosemite Falls, in Yosemite National Park is the tallest waterfall in North America

DINOSAUR

Scientists called **paleontologists** (PAY lee ahn TAHL uh jists) study dinosaur fossils. Many different kinds of dinosaur fossils have been found. Scientists can figure out if dinosaurs were meat eaters or plant eaters and if they were big or small.

The **brachiosaurus** (BRAY kee uh sawr us), the largest and tallest of all dinosaurs, lived 150 million years ago.The Brachiosaurus had long front legs and a long neck, which enabled it to eat tall plants.

The brachiosaurus may have been over 70 feet long and 40 feet tall, weighing more than 160,000 pounds!

These fossil bones are 145 million years old

BRIDGE

San Francisco is famous for many things; among them is the Golden Gate Bridge. The bridge towers rise 746 feet above the water. They are the tallest bridge towers in the world.

Golden Gate Bridge is a **suspension** (suh SPEN shun) bridge connecting San Francisco to Marin County, California. The center span of the bridge is 4,200 feet long. The Golden Gate Strait, a waterway that separates San Francisco Bay from the Pacific Ocean, runs 220 feet below.

Golden Gate Bridge has the tallest bridge towers in the world

Guinness World R

SAND SCULPTURE

Harrison Hot Springs is a small village in Canada that is famous for its sand sculptures.

The Sand Sculpture Society hosts a world competition every September. In 1993 a three-man team constructed the tallest sand castle in the world.

The "Christmas Tree" sand sculpture was made using only hands, buckets, and shovels. The real-looking Christmas tree stood over 21 feet.

TREE

Redwood trees are among the tallest of all living things. The coast redwood, which grows along the Pacific Coast of the United States, can grow up to 380 feet tall.

The giant **sequoia** (si KWOI uh), another species of redwood, is the most massive of all living things. Some may weigh over five million pounds!

Redwood trees are also among the oldest living things. Some redwoods may be more than 3,000 years old. Redwoods live so long and grow so tall because their wood is **resistant** (ri ZIS tunt) to insects and fire.

This woman looks small standing at the base of a giant redwood tree

WATERFALL

Thousands of waterfalls crown hundreds of rivers around the world. The tallest waterfall in North America is **Yosemite** (yo SEM eh tee) Falls in Yosemite National Park.

Yosemite Falls is divided into three sections. The three sections combine for a total drop of 2,425 feet.

When snow melts in the spring or when heavy rains wash into Yosemite Creek, the falls roar to life. During dry periods the falls slow to a trickle.

Glossary

brachiosaurus (BRAY kee uh sawr us) — a dinosaur that lived in the late Jurassic Period, 150 million years ago

paleontologists (PAY lee ahn TAHL uh jists) — scientists who study fossil remains

sequoia (si KWOI uh) — the largest kind of redwood tree

suspension (suh SPEN shun) — hanging down without center support, as in a suspension bridge

resistant (ri ZIS tunt) — being able to oppose or fight against

Yosemite (yo SEM eh tee) — a national park and major waterfall in California

INDEX